YOUR KNOWLEDGE HAS VALUE

Maureen Ndavi

HSBC Banking and Finance

GRIN Verlag

Bibliografische Information der Deutschen Nationalbibliothek:

Die Deutsche Bibliothek verzeichnet diese Publikation in der Deutschen National-
bibliografie; detaillierte bibliografische Daten sind im Internet über http://dnb.d-
nb.de/ abrufbar.

Imprint:

Copyright © 2013 GRIN Verlag GmbH
Druck und Bindung: Books on Demand GmbH, Norderstedt Germany
ISBN: 978-3-656-63720-2

This book at GRIN:

http://www.grin.com/en/e-book/271481/hsbc-banking-and-finance

GRIN - Your knowledge has value

Der GRIN Verlag publiziert seit 1998 wissenschaftliche Arbeiten von Studenten, Hochschullehrern und anderen Akademikern als eBook und gedrucktes Buch. Die Verlagswebsite www.grin.com ist die ideale Plattform zur Veröffentlichung von Hausarbeiten, Abschlussarbeiten, wissenschaftlichen Aufsätzen, Dissertationen und Fachbüchern.

Visit us on the internet:

http://www.grin.com/

http://www.facebook.com/grincom

http://www.twitter.com/grin_com

Table of Contents

Introduction..2

Analyze the bank's profit performance for the period 2007-2011 using financial statements and ratios.....2

Ratio Analysis of HSBC for 2007-2011 2

Evaluation on how ROE is decomposed to measure HSBC performance....................................8

Evaluation of how the bank measures and manages its interest rate risk. 9

Main strategies adopted by the bank in recent years and their effect on the bank's core businesses 9

Recommendations to senior management about the potential issues that might affect profitability..........10

Recommendations to Manage Interest Rate Risk 11

How management could position the company strategically...11

Introduction

Financial sector has been one of the fastest growing sectors in the world. Due to heavy competition among leading financial organizations and uncertain market, it has become mandatory for every financial organization or bank to evaluate its financial performance and strategies against financial objectives. In this small research paper, as one of the members of HSBC's Asset and Liability Committee, I am going to assess the bank's performance of over the last four years. Some of the key aspects considered in this paper are analyzing some of its risk exposures and assessing the impact of the major strategic choices the bank has made. HSBC is one of the leading multinational banking and financial services organizations in the world. With the headquarters located in London, the United Kingdom, the bank has been operating around 7200 offices across 85 countries in the world (HSBC, 2011).

Analyze the bank's profit performance for the period 2007-2011 using financial statements and ratio analysis

Ratio analysis is one of the popular methods used to understand the relationship between various items in the financial statements as well as to understand the operational performance and financial position of an organization (Giacomino and Mielke, 1993).

Ratio Analysis of HSBC for 2007-2011

Ratio analysis can be divided into 4 major parts. They are Liquidity Ratios, Efficiency Ratios, Profitability Ratios and Solvency Ratios (Streuly, 1994). Liquidity ratios are used to understand the ability of the organization to meet the short term obligations. Profitability ratios are used to understand the ability of the organization to generate profits against costs and expenses. Efficiency ratios are used to understand the ability of the organization to manage the internal assets and liabilities. In the same way, solvency ratios are used to understand the ability of the organization to meet the long-term obligations (Giacomino and Mielke, 1993).

Net Profit Margin

Net Profit Margin = Net Profit after Tax/ Sales

The net profit margin ratio is calculated to determine the profitability of the organization, i.e. the net profit earned by the organization after paying interests and taxes (Giacomino and Mielke, 1993).

Net Profit Margin					
Year	2011	2010	2009	2008	2007
Net Profit After Tax	17,944.00	14,191.00	6,694.00	6,498.00	20,455.00
Sales	83,461.00	80,014.00	78,631.00	88,571.00	87,601.00
Net Profit Margin	0.21	0.18	0.09	0.07	0.23

In the financial year 2007, HSBC has recorded healthy net margin of around 23%. By looking at the trend of the net profit margin ratio of the organization from 2007 to 2009, it is apparent that the net profit has significantly gone down in financial years 2008 and 2009. The major reason behind this slump was the recent economic recession, which had significant impact on the global banking sector. The net profit margin ratios of HSBC for financial years of 2010 and 2011 have recorded as 18% and 21% respectively. This sudden jump in the net profit margin is attributed to the banking sector recovery.

Return on Assets

Return on Assets = Net Profit after Tax/ Total Assets.

Return on Assets ratio will help investors to understand the ability of the organization to acquire funds and deposits at a reasonable rate and distribute them to profitable investment portfolio (Streuly, 1994).

Return on Assets					
Year	2011	2010	2009	2008	2007
Net Profit	17,944.00	14,191.00	6,694.00	6,498.00	20,455.00
Total Assets	2,555,579.00	2,454,689.00	2,364,452.00	2,527,465.00	2,354,266.00
Return on Assets	0.0070	0.0058	0.0028	0.0026	0.0087

This ratio also shows how effectively the organization has used its assets to generate profits. The higher return on assets indicates higher profitability of the bank and vice versa. The analysis of return on assets of HSBC for 2007-2011 indicates that the organization has not been able to invest funds on profitable investments. The ROA ratios for financial years 2008 and 2009 show how HSBC has struggled to invest funds on profitable investments; HSBC has recorded ROA of 0.0028 and 0.0026 for 2008 and 2009 respectively.

Tax Burden

Tax Burden = Net Income / Pretax Income

Interest Burden shows the proportion of profits retained after paying tax (Giacomino and Mielke, 1993).

Tax Burden					
Year	2011	2010	2009	2008	2007
Net Income	17,944.00	14,191.00	6,694.00	6,498.00	20,455.00
Pretax Income	21,872.00	19,037.00	7,079.00	9,307.00	24,212.00
Net Income/Pretax Income	0.82	0.75	0.95	0.7	0.84

The tax burden of HSBC has been fluctuating for the five year period. The highest tax burden rate was recorded in 2009 majorly because of the low levels of operating revenues. The tax burden has increased by approximately 10% again from 2010 to 2011.

Interest Burden

Interest Burden = Pretax Income/EBIT

Interest Burden shows the proportion of profits retained after paying interest (Giacomino and Mielke, 1993).

Interest Burden					
Year	2011	2010	2009	2008	2007
Pretax Income	21,872.00	19,037.00	7,079.00	9,307.00	24,212.00
EBIT	18,608.00	16,520.00	5,298.00	7,646.00	22,709.00
Pretax Income/ EBIT	1.18	1.15	1.34	1.22	1.07

The interest burden ratios of HSBC have also been fluctuating for the five year period. In fact, the year, 2009, HSBC has recorded high interest burden compared to other years due to poor economic conditions as well as less operating revenues. The analysis also makes it clear that the interest burden has again increased from 2010 to 2011 by 20%.

Operating Income Margin

Operating Income Margin = EBIT/ Sales

Operating Income Margin shows the ability of the organization to generate profits from operations. Operating performance of an organization will be measured with the help of operating income margin (Streuly, 1994).

Operating Income Margin					
Year	2011	2010	2009	2008	2007
EBIT	18,608.00	16,520.00	5,298.00	7,646.00	22,709.00
Sales	83,461.00	80,014.00	78,631.00	88,571.00	87,601.00
EBIT/ Sales	0.22	0.21	0.07	0.09	0.26

In the financial year 200, HSBC has recorded healthy operating income of around 26%. By looking at the trend of the net profit margin ratio of the organization from 2007 to 2009, it is apparent that the net profit has significantly gone down in financial years 2008 and 2009 majorly due to poor economic conditions, which did not help HSBC to implement its plans perfectly. , The operating income margin ratios of HSBC for financial years of 2010 and 2011 have recorded as 0.21 and 0.22 respectively due to market recovery.

Total Asset Turnover Ratio

Total Asset Turnover Ratio = Sales / Total Assets

Total Asset Turnover Ratio will help people to determine the ability of the organization to use its assets towards generating huge revenues (Streuly, 1994).

Total Asset Turnover Ratio					
Year	2011	2010	2009	2008	2007
Sales	83,461.00	80,014.00	78,631.00	88,571.00	87,601.00
Total Assets	2,555,579.00	2,454,689.00	2,364,452.00	2,527,465.00	2,354,266.00
Sales/ Total Assets	0.03	0.03	0.03	0.04	0.04

Normally, asset turnover ratios will be used to check if the revenues of the organization are growing in proportion to the sales. The analysis has clearly indicated that HSBC has recoded similar ratios for all financial years in between 2007 and 2011. As the standard asset turnover ratio for banking industry is around 0.5%, it can be concluded that HSBC has not utilized its assets to generate sales revenues like other banks.

Return on Equity

Return on Equity = Net Income / Income before Tax * Income before Tax/EBIT * EBIT/ Sales *Sales / Total Assets * Assets/ Equity = Net Income/ Equity

Return on Equity ratio is used to measure the ability of the organization to generate the profit with the help of funds invested by shareholders (Williams et al, 2008)

Return on Equity Ratio					
Year	2011	2010	2009	2008	2007
Net Income	17,944.00	14,191.00	6,694.00	6,498.00	20,455.00
Equity	158,725.00	147,667.00	128,299.00	93,591.00	128,160.00
Net Income / Equity	0.11	0.1	0.05	0.07	0.16

In simple terms, ROE measures the growth potential as well as the profitability of the organization. HSBC has recorded ROE of 16%, 7%, 5%, 10% and 11% for financial years, 2007 to 2011 respectively. The ROE has decreased more than 100% from 2007 to 2008 majorly because of inability of the organization to handle the financial recession. After the recession, HSBC witnessed again 100% jump in ROE from 2009 to 2010. HSBC has the taken the advantage of market recovery to effectively generate profits with the help of funds invested by stakeholders.

Cost to Income Ratio

Cost to Income Ratio= Total Cost / Total Income

Cost to Income ratio is used to measure the income generated per unit cost. With the help of this ratio, it is also possible to understand how expensive for an organization to generate a unit of output (Giacomino and Mielke, 1993).

Cost to Income Ratio					
Year	2011	2010	2009	2008	2007
Cost	41,545.00	37,688.00	34,395.00	49,099.00	39,042.00
Sales	83,461.00	80,014.00	78,631.00	88,571.00	87,601.00
Total Cost/Total Income	0.5	0.47	0.44	0.55	0.45

With this ratio, in this context, one can measure the cost efficiency levels of HSBC. The results show that the cost efficiency of the organization is stable for all five financial years. While it has touched its lowest figure, 44%, in 2009, it has reached its highest figure, %55 in 2008. Overall, the Cost to Income ratio of HSBC has oscillated in between 044 to 0.55. The results also show that the recent financial downturn did not influence the operational efficient of the organization very much.

Earnings per Share

Earnings per share will be calculated to determine how well an organization is performing in the trade markets (Giacomino and Mielke, 1993).

Earning per Share					
Year	2011	2010	2009	2008	2007
Basic earnings per share	0.92	0.73	0.34	0.41	1.44
Diluted earnings per share	0.91	0.72	0.34	0.41	1.42

With this ratio, investors will be able to understand the profit allocated to each outstanding share. If the trend of earning per share is increasing, it is considered that the performance of the organization is good and vice versa. When it comes to the earning per share ratio of HSBC, the recorded figures are $0.44, $0.41, $0.31, $0.73, $0.92. The comparative analysis made it clear that HSBC has bounced back in the market after the financial downturn by recording an increased earning per ratio of around 130% from 2009 to 2010.

Overall, the performance of HSBC was not stable in the period between 2007 and 2011. Due to the financial recession in 2008, the performance of the organization has dropped to major extent and bounced back in 2010 due to market recovery. Though the figures recorded for ROA, ROE, Leverage and Asset Turnover are encouraging for 2010 and 2011, it is very important for HSBC to make sure that organization will make use of assets and equity impeccably to generate more profits. Though the cost to Income ratio is stable, the top management of the organization should take steps towards reducing the expenses required to generate unit cost of output.

Evaluation on how ROE is decomposed to measure HSBC performance

Return on Equity ratio is used to evaluate the rate of return to the shareholder's equity. In simple terms, the ROE shows the net income retuned by an organization as a percentage of the shareholder's equity. DuPont analysis is one of the popular methods used to decompose the ROE into various parts (Zane at al, 2004). The decomposition also presents several ratios which are used to measure the performance of the organization by fundamental analysis. With the decomposition, ROE can be divided into five major ratios. These ratios include Interest burden, Operating Income Margin, Asset Turnover, Tax Burden and Leverage Ratio. The combination all these above ratios will form ROE of an organization (Zane at al, 2004).

For different industries, ROE will be influenced due to any above ratios. For instance, industries such as retail stores, which record lesser margin rates and leverage rates, the ROE will be majorly influenced by ratios such as asset turnover ratio and return on asset ratio. For industries that operate on high margins, the ROE will be majorly influenced due to net profit margin and sales turnover. Organizations that sell apparels and fashion goods are perfect examples for high margin industries. Similarly, HSBC belongs to industries which are known for high leverage. For these kinds of industries, leverage ratio will influence the ROE; high leverage ratio will generate reasonable ROE rates for financial industries (Zane at al, 2004).

While decomposing the ROE ratio, it is important to calculate tax burden and interest burden on the organization because both interest and tax play a huge role in influencing profit of the organization. The only reason behind ROE decomposition is to understand which part of the ratio is influencing the ROE. The tax burden of HSBC has been fluctuating for the five year period. The highest tax burden rate was recorded in 2009 majorly because of the low levels of operating revenues. The interest burden ratios of HSBC have been stable for last five years. In fact, the year, 2009, HSBC has recorded less interest burden compared to other years. The major component of ROE analysis of HSBC is the leverage ratio. In accordance with the claims of experts that financial institutions record high leverage ratios, HSBC has been recording high leverage ratios since 2007. For every financial year, assets of the HSBC are more the 16 times of the equity generated from the shareholders.

Evaluation of how the bank measures and manages its interest rate risk.

Interest rate risk is nothing but the sudden changes in interest rate that may reduce the profitability of the organization (Phillipe, 2001). For HSBC, the interest rate risk arises from various sources. The first and foremost interest rate risk arises due to timing differences in reprising assets and liabilities of the organization; this risk is more common for organizations that borrow funds for short-term to invest on long-term assets and vice versa. The second major interest rate risk arises due to rate differences of amounts paid and earned; if interest rates change suddenly, banks will witness huge differences cash flows and earnings (Phillipe, 2001). The interest rate risk that rose due to rate differences in amounts paid and earned is called as basis risk. In the international markets, the third and most dangerous interest rate risk arises due to existence of options in portfolio of assets, liabilities and other off-balance sheet instruments.

HSBC has been using a well-known technique called, Maturity & Reprising Model, to measure and manage interest rate risk (Phillipe, 2001). With the help of the Maturity & Reprising Model, the officials of HSBC will try to distribute assets, liabilities and other non-balance sheet items in a table based on the time remaining for the maturity as well as reprising. As it is common that some assets and liabilities in the table may not have clear reprising intervals, these assets and liabilities are reprised based on the capability of the bank to amend interest rates in future. Once the table is developed, it will act as the perfect indicator to measure the interest rate risk for the organization (Phillipe, 2001).

Main strategies adopted by the bank in recent years and their effect on the bank's core businesses

HSBC has been implementing wide-range of strategies to become the world's leading international bank.

- Some of the strategies used by HSBC in recent years are (HSBC, 2011):
- Focusing on current trends
- Reshaping the entire group to close non-strategic businesses
- Focusing on fastest growing regions such as China, India and Malaysia
- Business expansion in commercial banking

All these above strategies have given positive results for HSBC in last couple of years. With the help of the strategy, focusing on current trends, HSBC has been doing incredibly great business in international trade. The cash flows from the international trade have significantly in the financial year, 2011 (HSBC, 2011). By going according to the trend, HSBC has also been focusing on wealth creating in fastest growing markets such as China and India with pure focus on retail sector.

In the financial year, 2010, the organization has conducted a review on existing services and businesses. After the review of group portfolio, the organization has taken the decision to close around 16 non-strategic businesses to improve the efficiency of the capital deployment. Due to this strategy, the organization was able to achieve the return on equity around 10% in 2010 and 11% in 2011. The organization has targeted 15% of return on equity for 2012 and 2013 (HSBC, 2011).

The strategy, 'Focusing on fastest growing regions' helped HSBC to record high growth rates in countries like China, Brazil, Mexico and Singapore (HSBC, 2011). The revenues from these fastest growing regions have increased by 24% in 2011. In the same way, the strategy of focusing more commercial banking has also fetched humongous results for HSBC. HSBC has witnessed around 31% of growth from 2010 to 2011 in the commercial banking region. With this, HSBC has become one of the leading providers of commercial banking services in the world (HSBC, 2011).

Recommendations to senior management about the potential issues that might affect profitability

In today's competitive environment, it is important for any bank to recognize potential issues that may affect profitability so that the management can take the proactive measures. Some of the potential issues that may impact profitability include:

1. Impending economic recessions and changing economic conditions – It is recommended to the officials of the bank to keep an update on regular trends in the market. It will help them to recognize any impending changes in economic conditions well in advance. If these changes are recognized well in advance, it is not a big deal to implement strategies that counter poor economic conditions.

2. Competitive behavior within the industry – A market analysis on competitor' strategies, interest rate policies and investment policies would help HSBC to counter the competition within the market.

3. Inflation in the market–Apparently, HSBC should keep an eye on inflation work on appropriate savings rate and lending rate so that the profitability will not be impacted.

4. Regulatory conditions – It is recommended to strictly adhere to the regulatory mechanisms because most of the times, the profitability of the banks will be affected to fines imposed by regulatory bodes for not adhering to regulations.

Recommendations to Manage Interest Rate Risk

It is recommended to the officials of HSBC to use latest software applications that give information on maturity and reprising values of assets, liabilities as well as future investments so that the interest rate risk could be minimized. In the same way, with the help of Simulation Model, the officials of the bank will consider wide range of interest rate scenarios and corresponding cash flows so that it is possible for them to understand the range of interest rate changes (Phillipe, 2001). Generally, organizations will include assets and liabilities which are presented in the balance sheet as well as the possible new investments in the simulation model. Though simulation model takes good software applications and resources, large scale banks such as HSBC can afford to use it for measuring and managing interest rate risk.

How management could position the company strategically

As HSBC has been trying to focus on commercial banking, it is recommended to the top management of HSBC to position the bank leading commercial bank rather than focusing on Retail Bankingand Wealth Management. As the bank is already an established player in Retail Bankingand Wealth Management, it can generate business irrespective of the promotion in retail banking segment. Moreover, in developing counties like China, India and Mexico, commercial banking has huge scope.

References

Giacomino, D.E. and Mielke, D.E, 1993. Cash Flows: Another Approach to Ratio Analysis. Journal of Accountancy 175, 55-8.

HSBC, 2011. HSBC Annual Report. Retrieved on 13th February from <http://www.hsbc.com/investor-relations/financial-results>

Phillipe, J., 2001. Value-at-Risk: The New Benchmark for Managing Financial Risk. 2nd edition, New York: McGraw-Hill.

Streuly, A.C., 1994.The Primary Objective Of Financial Reporting: How Are We Doing? The Ohio CPA Journal 53, 15-22

Williams, J. R., Susan F. H., Mark S. B. and Joseph V. C., 2008. Financial & Managerial Accounting. McGraw-Hill Irwin. pp. 266.

Zane, B., Kane, A. and Marcus, A. J., 2004. Essentials of Investments, 5th ed. McGraw-Hill Irwin. p. 460.